FOURQUEMIN
DERRIEN

MISS ENDICOTT

PART I

CINEBOOK
EXPRESSO

Original title: Miss Endicott – Tome 1
Original edition: © Editions du Lombard (Dargaud-Lombard s.a.) 2014 by Fourquemin and Derrien
Colours: Scarlett
www.lelombard.com
English translation: © 2019 Cinebook Ltd
Translator: Jerome Saincantin
Editor: Erica Olson Jeffrey
Lettering and text layout: Design Amorandi
Printed in Spain by EGEDSA
This edition first published in Great Britain in 2021 by
Cinebook Ltd
56 Beech Avenue
Canterbury, Kent
CT4 7TA
www.cinebook.com
A CIP catalogue record for this book
is available from the British Library
ISBN 978-1-84918-544-8

WE ARE GATHERED HERE TO PAY HOMAGE TO OUR FRIEND AND KINSWOMAN, MARGUERITE MADELEINE ENDICOTT ...

... THOUGH, TO ALL OF US, SHE WILL ALWAYS BE 'OUR MAGGIE'.

ALWAYS READY TO HELP THE POOR.

WE'VE ALL NEEDED HER AT SOME POINT.

1

3

MISS ENDICOTT?

YOU'RE MAGGIE'S DAUGHTER, AREN'T YOU?

YES, I AM.

SOME WOMAN, YOUR MOTHER WAS!

I KNOW!

I DIDN'T SEE YOU WITH HER OFTEN.

WELL ... I'M JUST BACK FROM A LONG JOURNEY!

MAGGIE LEFT THIS KEY WITH ME SHORTLY BEFORE SHE PASSED ...

YOU SHOULD KNOW WHICH DOOR IT OPENS!

ALL THE BEST, MISS ENDICOTT!

2

MISS ENDICOTT, I PRESUME?

IT FALLS TO ME TO WELCOME YOU TODAY.

THE FOLSEYS ARE OUT THIS MORNING ... THEY'RE NOT OFTEN HERE, AS YOU'LL SEE ...

... THEY ARE RATHER BUSY PEOPLE!

3

I MUST WARN YOU: THIS NANNY POSITION IS OFTEN VACANT. YOUNG MASTER EVAN IS SOMEWHAT ... MISCHIEVOUS!

I'M SURE YOU'LL MANAGE TO WIN HIM OVER, THOUGH ... AT LEAST, I HOPE SO, FOR YOUR SAKE.

YOU'LL HAVE THE RUN OF THE WHOLE MANSION, EXCEPT FOR SIR'S OFFICE.

HE KEEPS HIS EROTIC WOOD-BLOCK PRINTS THERE ...

... THOSE HE IMPORTS FROM JAPAN!

THIS IS YOUR ROOM. SMALL, HUMBLE. BE GLAD OF IT — YOU HAVEN'T SEEN MINE! ...

... ANY QUESTIONS, MISS ENDICOTT?

PRUDENCE. CALL ME PRUDENCE. WILL I BE ALLOWED TO LEAVE AT NIGHT SOMETIMES? ...

... AFTER DINNER?

AT YOUR OWN PERIL. THE NEIGHBOURHOOD ISN'T ESPECIALLY SAFE AFTER DARK, BUT YOU ARE YOUR OWN MISTRESS ONCE EVAN IS IN BED!!

UNTIL LATER, PRUDENCE ... I'M CONRAD.

4

KNOCK
KNOCK

IT'S DINNERTIME.

I'M COMING!

GOOD EVENING, EVAN.

DO YOU LIKE WELSH RAREBIT? ... IT'S MY FAVOURITE DISH!

5

I WOULDN'T EAT IT EVERY DAY. I DO LOVE CURRIED RICE, THOUGH!

AND LEMON JELLY ... I CAN'T GET ENOUGH OF IT!!

WHO CHOOSES THE MENU IN THIS HOUSE?

OH, FATHER AND MOTHER DON'T EAT HERE OFTEN ...

SIMONE, THE COOK, TAKES CARE OF EVERYTHING! ...

... JUST SO YOU KNOW, AVOID HER OLIVE BREAD IF YOU VALUE YOUR TEETH!

AHEM ... I HAVE TO ADMIT THAT MASTER EVAN ISN'T ENTIRELY WRONG ABOUT THAT!

HMM ... VERY WELL. LET'S MAKE A DEAL, EVAN ... FROM TOMORROW ON, I'LL BE OVERSEEING YOUR EDUCATION.

IF YOU PAY ATTENTION TO YOUR CLASSES AND MAKE GOOD PROGRESS, I'LL TALK TO SIMONE ...

... SO THAT SHE'LL MAKE YOU YOUR FAVOURITE DISHES FROM TIME TO TIME ... HOW DOES THAT SOUND?

6

ALL RIGHT!!

EXCELLENT... NOW IT'S TIME FOR YOU TO GO TO BED!

IS SOMETHING THE MATTER, CONRAD?

IT'S JUST THAT... USUALLY, THE NEW NANNIES DON'T EVEN LAST THE FIRST NIGHT...

WHY?! HE'S ADORABLE!

THAT'S THE STRANGEST PART! YOU SEEM TO HAVE CHARMED HIM. HE'S LIKE A DIFFERENT CHILD.

I DEARLY HOPE IT LASTS!

ARE YOU SURE YOU WANT TO GO OUT ALONE TONIGHT?

I HAVE TO!

I'LL BE QUIET WHEN I COME BACK!

7

OOOH, LOOK AT THE PRETTY LADY ...

HER SKIN MUST BE SO SOFT ... SHE LOOKS SCRUMPTIOUS!

8

DARREN EMERSON! YOU'RE A LECHEROUS PIG!!

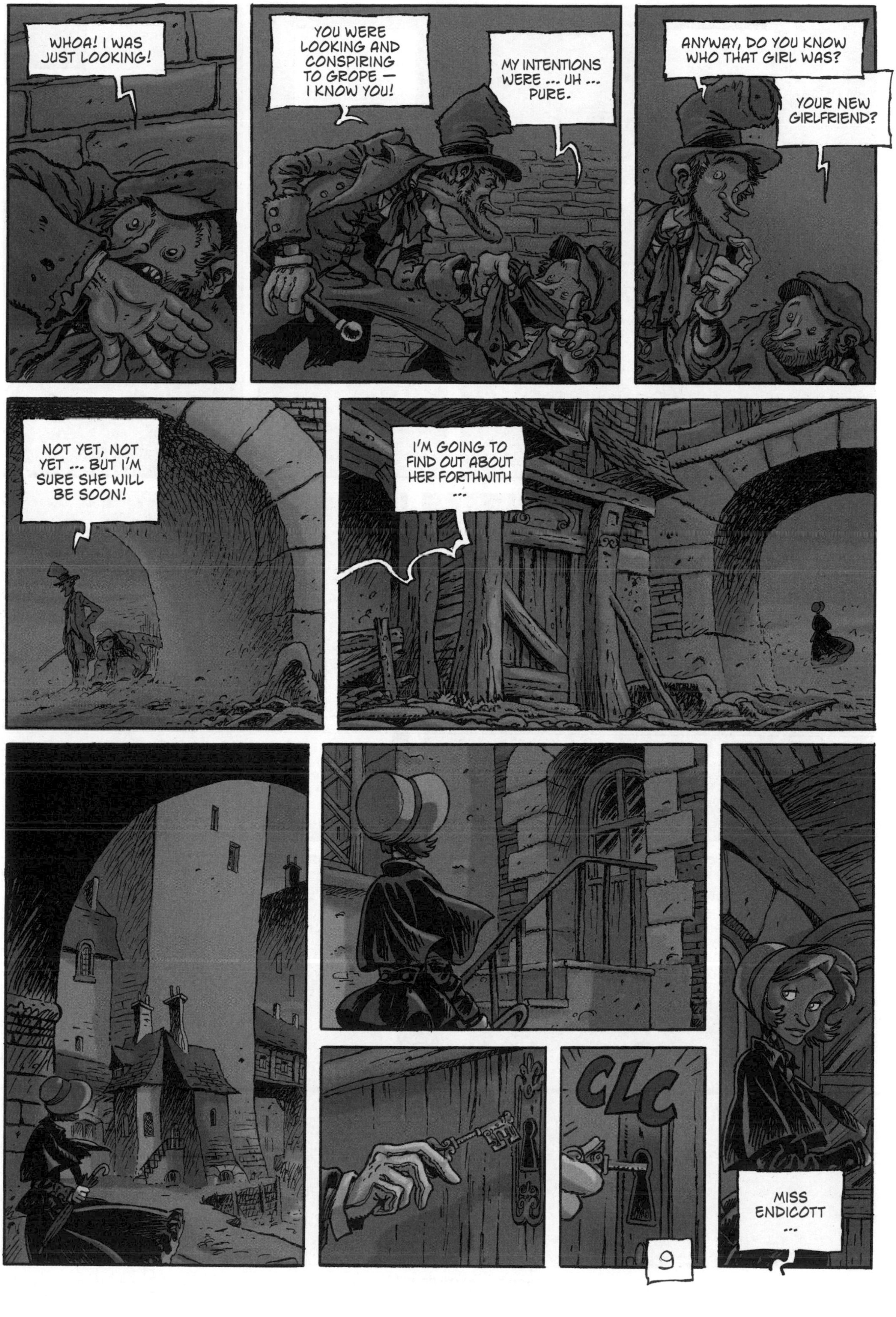
WHOA! I WAS JUST LOOKING!
YOU WERE LOOKING AND CONSPIRING TO GROPE — I KNOW YOU!
MY INTENTIONS WERE ... UH ... PURE.
ANYWAY, DO YOU KNOW WHO THAT GIRL WAS?
YOUR NEW GIRLFRIEND?
NOT YET, NOT YET ... BUT I'M SURE SHE WILL BE SOON!
I'M GOING TO FIND OUT ABOUT HER FORTHWITH ...
CLC
MISS ENDICOTT ...
9

YOU MUST BE WALLACE ...

I AM INDEED. YOUR PERSONAL SECRETARY, NOW.

I DIDN'T SEE YOU AT THE FUNERAL ...

I COULDN'T. IT WAS SIMPLY TOO PAINFUL.

MY GOODNESS! YOU DON'T CLEAN VERY OFTEN IN HERE.

THAT'S NOT ONE OF MY DUTIES, MISS PRUDENCE!

WELL, IT WILL BE FROM NOW ON ... RIGHT NOW, IN FACT!

MISS MARGUERITE NEVER ASKED ANYTHING OF THE SORT OF ME.

NEW CONCILIATOR, NEW HABITS!

KNOCK

KNOCK

OH! ALREADY A FIRST PETITION?

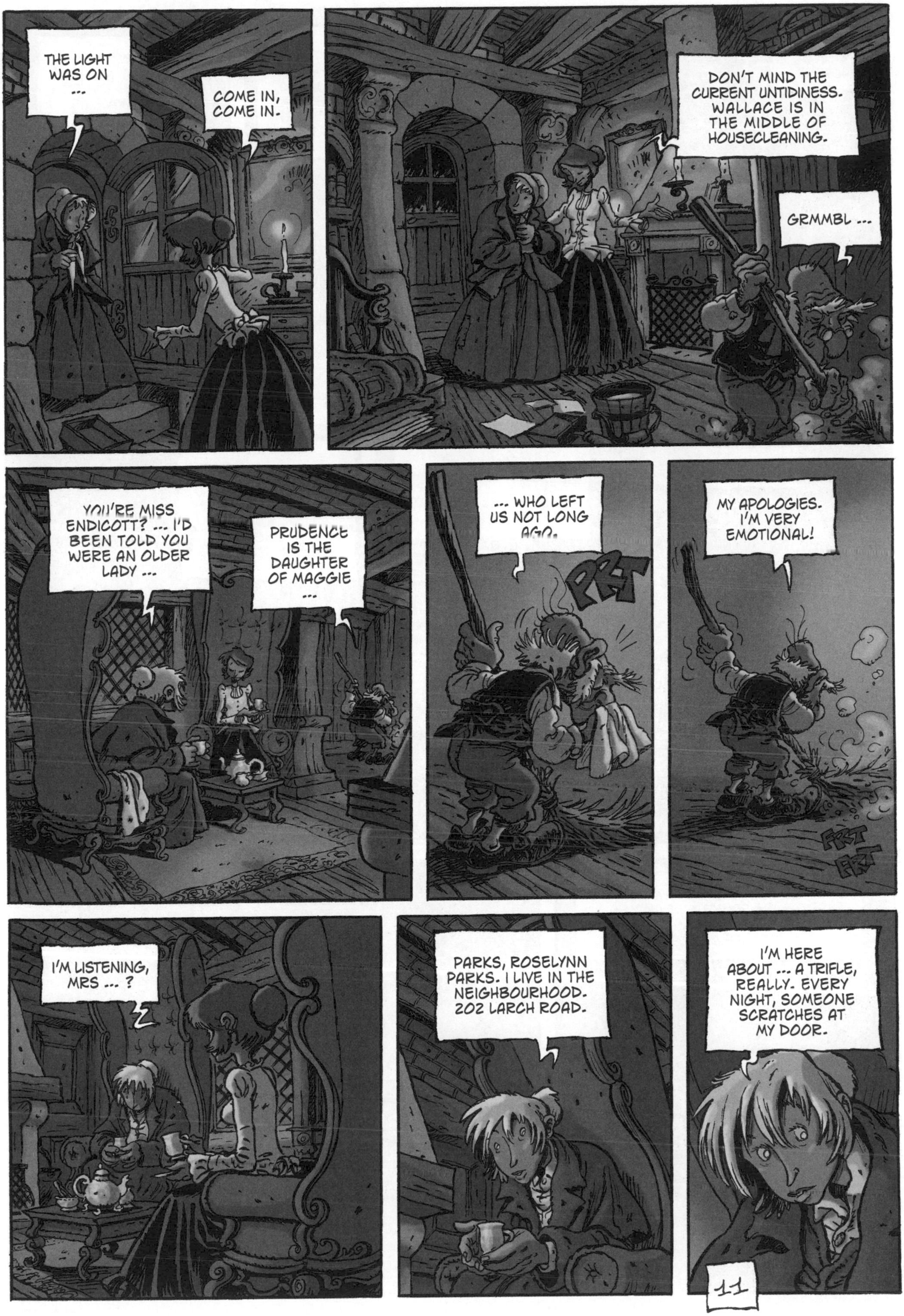
THE LIGHT WAS ON ...
COME IN, COME IN.
DON'T MIND THE CURRENT UNTIDINESS. WALLACE IS IN THE MIDDLE OF HOUSECLEANING.
GRMMBL ...
YOU'RE MISS ENDICOTT? ... I'D BEEN TOLD YOU WERE AN OLDER LADY ...
PRUDENCE IS THE DAUGHTER OF MAGGIE ...
... WHO LEFT US NOT LONG AGO.
PRT
MY APOLOGIES. I'M VERY EMOTIONAL!
FRT
FRT
I'M LISTENING, MRS ... ?
PARKS, ROSELYNN PARKS. I LIVE IN THE NEIGHBOURHOOD. 202 LARCH ROAD.
I'M HERE ABOUT ... A TRIFLE, REALLY. EVERY NIGHT, SOMEONE SCRATCHES AT MY DOOR.
11

COME AGAIN?

YES. EVERY NIGHT, AT PRECISELY ONE O'CLOCK ... OH, NOT FOR LONG! JUST A FEW MINUTES. BUT NEITHER I NOR MY HUSBAND HAVE DARED OPEN THE DOOR ...

I STRONGLY SUSPECT QUILBY'S GANG OF WANTING TO SHAKE US DOWN ...

QUILBY?

THE LOCAL CRIME BOSS. MISS MARGUERITE KNEW HIM WELL. THERE WAS MUTUAL RESPECT BETWEEN THEM!

WE DON'T HAVE ANY MORE MONEY TO GIVE THEM. TIMES ARE TOUGH. SOMEONE SUGGESTED I COME TO YOU.

YOU DID THE RIGHT THING!

I'LL TAKE CARE OF YOUR PROBLEM TONIGHT ... AND — THIS GOES WITHOUT SAYING — FREE OF CHARGE.

GO HOME, MRS PARKS, AND DON'T WORRY!

12

WHAT DO YOU THINK, WALLACE?

?

YOU'RE INTERESTED IN MY OPINION?

YOU HAVE BEEN HERE MUCH LONGER THAN I.

QUILBY ... I KNEW HIM WHEN HE WAS A LAD ... HE WASN'T SUCH A BAD SORT ...

... THEN HE WENT ASTRAY. THESE DAYS HE'S CAPABLE OF ANYTHING ... THE WORST AND THE UNTHINKABLE!

CLAP

GOING BACK TO THE POSH NEIGHBOUR-HOODS?

I'M OFF TO MEET THIS QUILBY!

YOU'LL FIND HIM AT PATTERSON'S TONIGHT. YOU'RE MAD ... LIKE YOUR LATE MOTHER WAS!

I WOULDN'T BE PICKING UP THE TORCH OTHERWISE.

CLAP

YOU'LL HAVE TO IMPROVE THOSE PUBLIC RELATIONS, MISS ENDICOTT ...

... I FOUND YOU SOMEWHAT AVERAGE ...

13

YOUR FUTURE SWEETHEART'S GOING TO PATTERSON'S ... IN THE MIDDLE OF THE NIGHT?

I COULD TELL SHE WAS A FEISTY ONE!!

AHEM ...

?

UH ... THIS ISN'T REALLY A PLACE FOR A LADY LIKE YOU!

THANK YOU, BUT I DON'T HAVE A CHOICE. I HAVE AN APPOINTMENT INSIDE WITH A SUPPOSEDLY IMPORTANT MAN!

ARE YOU CERTAIN?

ABSOLUTELY!

14

SLUMMING IT, ARE WE, M'LADY?

I'M LOOKING FOR ONE QUILBY. DO YOU WORK FOR HIM?

QUILBY ... Q ... U ... I ... L ... B ... Y!

AND WHAT DO YOU WANT WITH THIS QUILBY?

?

HE'S SHAKING DOWN SOMEONE I KNOW. I'D LIKE HIM TO STOP — RIGHT AWAY!

YOU'RE PRETTY QUICK TO ACCUSE THE GENTLEMAN. HE MIGHT TAKE UMBRAGE ...

15

I DON'T CARE ... AS LONG AS HE STOPS WHAT HE'S DOING IMMEDIATELY ...

OR WHAT?

OR I WILL DEAL WITH HIM!

I MEAN IT!

YOU'RE A PRETTY ONE, BUT IF YOU WEREN'T A WOMAN, I'D TEACH YOU A GOOD LESSON WITH MY FISTS!

OH, DON'T LET THAT HOLD YOU BACK. GO AHEAD!!

?

16

18

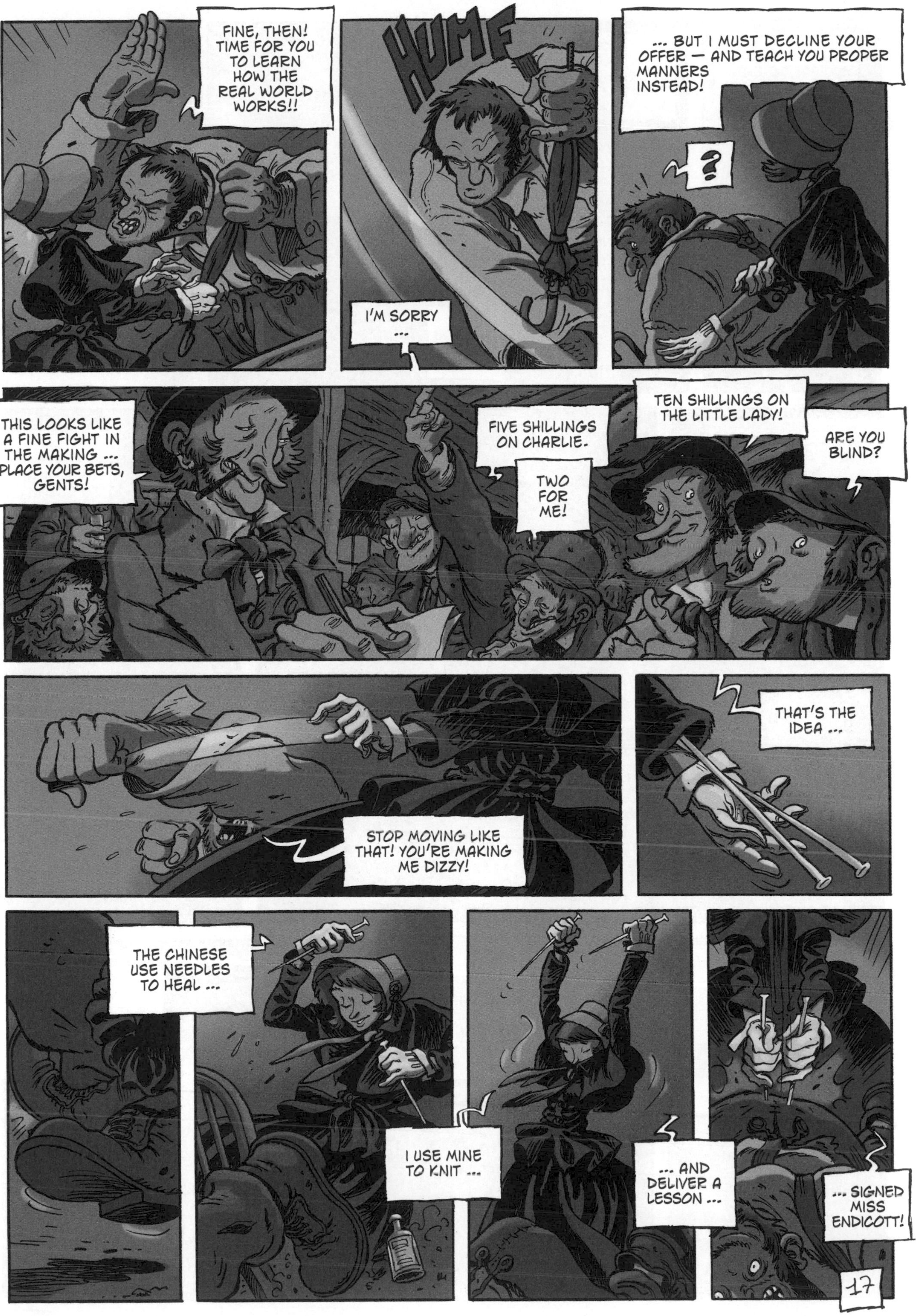
FINE, THEN! TIME FOR YOU TO LEARN HOW THE REAL WORLD WORKS!!
HUMF
I'M SORRY ...
... BUT I MUST DECLINE YOUR OFFER — AND TEACH YOU PROPER MANNERS INSTEAD!
?
THIS LOOKS LIKE A FINE FIGHT IN THE MAKING ... PLACE YOUR BETS, GENTS!
FIVE SHILLINGS ON CHARLIE.
TWO FOR ME!
TEN SHILLINGS ON THE LITTLE LADY!
ARE YOU BLIND?
STOP MOVING LIKE THAT! YOU'RE MAKING ME DIZZY!
THAT'S THE IDEA ...
THE CHINESE USE NEEDLES TO HEAL ...
I USE MINE TO KNIT ...
... AND DELIVER A LESSON ...
... SIGNED MISS ENDICOTT!
17

OH, WHY DIDN'T YOU SAY SO RIGHT AWAY?

YOU MUST BE MARGUERITE'S DAUGHTER. I SHOULD HAVE GUESSED FROM YOUR LOOKS.

ARE YOU QUILBY?

IN THE PROVERBIAL FLESH. MY FRIENDS CALL ME CUBBY, THOUGH.

I HAVE NO REASON TO BE YOUR FRIEND, FOR NOW!

IF YOU'LL COME WITH ME TO MY MEETING ROOM ...

A CUP OF TEA, PERHAPS? GREEN TEA? DARJEELING?

I DON'T CARE.

I'M NOT HERE TO SOCIALISE. I CAME TO SETTLE THE PARKSES' SITUATION!

I HEARD, AND I UNDERSTAND YOUR REASONING IN COMING HERE ...

YES?

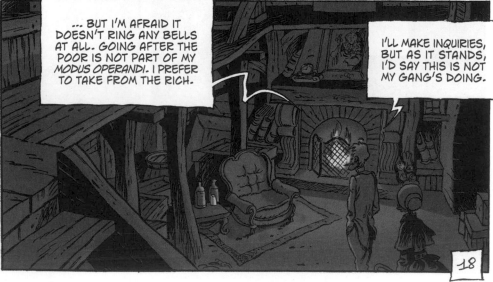

... BUT I'M AFRAID IT DOESN'T RING ANY BELLS AT ALL. GOING AFTER THE POOR IS NOT PART OF MY MODUS OPERANDI. I PREFER TO TAKE FROM THE RICH.

I'LL MAKE INQUIRIES, BUT AS IT STANDS, I'D SAY THIS IS NOT MY GANG'S DOING.

18

I'M NOT SURE WHY, BUT I BELIEVE YOU.

I DO HAVE AN UNFORTUNATE TENDENCY TO LIE TO PEOPLE ...

... BUT NOT TO MARGUERITE'S DAUGHTER. I WOULDN'T DARE!

KEEP ME APPRISED IF YOU HEAR ANYTHING ABOUT THIS BUSINESS!

I SHALL DO SO!

WHERE IS SHE BURIED?

CRIMSON HILL CEMETERY.

I WILL MAKE SURE THERE ARE ALWAYS FLOWERS ON HER GRAVE, EVEN IN WINTER ...

... FOR OLD TIMES' SAKE!

WE'RE RICH! WE'RE RICH!

CORRECTION: I AM RICH!!

HUMF!

I DO BELIEVE I BET ON THE RIGHT FILLY!

DID YOU ENJOY THE ATMOSPHERE?

I'VE NEVER HAD SO MUCH FUN ...

DO YOU HAVE THE TIME, PLEASE?

OF COURSE, MISS ...

IT'S ALMOST ONE IN THE MORNING!

PERFECT! TIME TO GO AND STAND MY FIRST WATCH.

NEVER JUDGE A BOOK BY ITS COVER!

20

HEY ... H ... HELLO, PRETT—HIC! ... L ... LADY!

S ... SO, SHW ... SWEETIE ... HOW MUCH?

HIC!

NOTHING — AND NEVER WITH YOU!

OH! SNOOTY!

DONG

HIC!

AH! IT'S TIME FOR THE SCRATCHING!

TIME FOR WHAT NOW?

I'LL LEAVE YOU TO SLEEP IT OFF.

SCRATT
SCRATT

SCRA

FOR THAT!

HEY!

SCRT
SCRT

21

Y ...YES?

MRS PARKS? IT'S MISS ENDICOTT. DON'T WORRY. I'M ON THE CASE!

WELL, TIME FOR ME TO GO, NOW!

WHAT'S GOING ON?

GO BACK TO SLEEP, DARLING! IT'S THE YOUNG WOMAN I TOLD YOU ABOUT ...

OH? WHY'D SHE WAKE US UP?

22

PRUDENCE? BREAKFAST IS SERVED ...

YOU LOOK TIRED, MISS ENDICOTT.

...

I ALWAYS HAVE TROUBLE SLEEPING THE FIRST FEW NIGHTS IN A NEW PLACE.

AH.

THIS PORRIDGE IS RATHER ... CRUNCHY!

REMEMBER THE OLIVE BREAD ...

I REALLY NEED TO HAVE A WORD WITH SIMONE!

WHY DON'T THE TWO OF US GO TO THE PARK?

HOW LONG HAS IT BEEN SINCE YOU SAW YOUR PARENTS?

OH, UH, I'M NOT REALLY SURE! ...

A WEEK, MAYBE? I WAS ABOUT TO GET BORED WHEN YOU ARRIVED!

AFTER THIS WALK, WE'RE GOING TO START IN EARNEST ON YOUR STUDIES.

I THOUGHT SO!

BY THE WAY, WHERE WERE YOU COMING FROM LAST NIGHT AT TWO O'CLOCK?

WELL ... I MEAN ...

NO WONDER YOU'RE TIRED THIS MORNING!

THIS IS RATHER INDISCREET OF YOU, EVAN!

NONETHELESS, I WILL ANSWER YOU.

MY MOTHER JUST PASSED AWAY. I HAD TO TAKE CARE OF SOME URGENT BUSINESS!

I SHOULDN'T HAVE ASKED YOU. I APOLO-GISE.

HOWEVER, IT IS **NOT** ALL RIGHT THAT YOU SHOULD STILL BE AWAKE AT TWO IN THE MORNING ... I'LL TALK TO CONRAD!

IT'S ALL RIGHT ...

OH, NO!

24

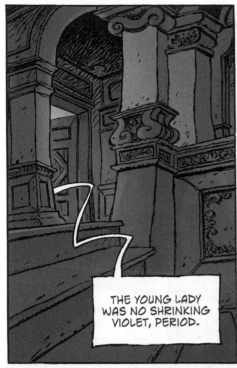

SHE PLANTED BOTH NEEDLES IN THE MISCREANT'S FUNDAMENT ...

NOT SO FAST!

THE YOUNG LADY WAS NO SHRINKING VIOLET, PERIOD.

SHE ... PLANTED ... BOTH ... NEEDLES ... IN THE MISCREANT'S ... FUNDAMENT ...

... IN FRONT OF EVERY ONE OF THE PUB'S REGULARS, FULL STOP.

ALL RIGHT, THAT'S ENOUGH FOR TODAY. I'LL MARK YOUR COPY. YOU CAN GO AND PLAY IN YOUR ROOM — I NEED TO GO SHOPPING.

THANKS, MISS ENDICOTT!

I'VE NEVER SEEN HIM ENJOY DICTATION SO MUCH!

WELL, I DID STRAY FROM THE CLASSICS SOMEWHAT!

25

YOU'RE A GOOD PERSON, PRUDENCE.

27

TONIGHT'S DINNER, APPARENTLY ...

... IS SUSPICIOUS SOUP AND ... SNIFF ... MYSTERY STEW! ...

... WHAT A FEAST ...

SHEESH KEBAB AND BASMATI RICE!

?

?

NOT A WORD TO SIMONE. SHE MUSTN'T KNOW ABOUT MY COOKING!

DID YOU REALLY MAKE IT YOURSELF?

I LEARNT A LOT ON MY TRAVELS.

THIS IS RATHER GOOD. YOU SHOULD TRY IT, CONRAD.

PLEASE DO! TAKE A PLATE, CONRAD.

THIS IS HARDLY PROPER ...

... BUT I MUST SAY I AM FAMISHED.

WE'RE MISSING SOME MUSIC!

26

WELL, THAT'S ALL FOR TONIGHT. DID YOU LIKE IT?

IT WAS DELICIOUS ... IS THERE ANY LEFT?

LOVELY!

NOW THAT EVAN IS IN BED, I HAVE TO GO ... I SHOULDN'T BE LONG.

I KNOW WHAT YOU DO, PRUDENCE ... I KNOW WHY YOU HAVE TO LEAVE EVERY NIGHT.

MARGUERITE ONCE HELPED ME FIND MY LOST SISTER!

I WON'T SAY A WORD OF YOUR DOUBLE LIFE TO ANYONE.

YOU'RE A GOOD PERSON TOO, CONRAD!

27

SO, DID QUILBY CONFESS?

I NEED A PICKAXE, A MAP OF THE NEIGHBOURHOOD'S CELLARS, AND A CUP OF TEA! ...

IN THAT ORDER?

I WANT TO SOLVE THIS CASE AS QUICKLY AS POSSIBLE!

AH, YES ... THE THREAT TO THE PARKSES' SLEEP IS DIRE!

YOU'LL FIND ALL THE MAPS YOU'LL NEED IN THIS ... BY THE WAY, DID YOU ENJOY INDIA?

?

YOU KNOW A LOT ABOUT ME!

MISS MARGUERITE OFTEN SPOKE OF YOU ...

I'M SORRY, BUT I FIND IT DIFFICULT TO CONCENTRATE ON MY READING.

WALLACE ... DOES THE 'WORLD OF THE FORGOTTEN' MEAN ANYTHING TO YOU?

IT'S A FAIRY TALE. JUST LIKE MY PAYMENTS FOR SERVICES RENDERED.

RIGHT. TIME TO GO!

CLAP

28

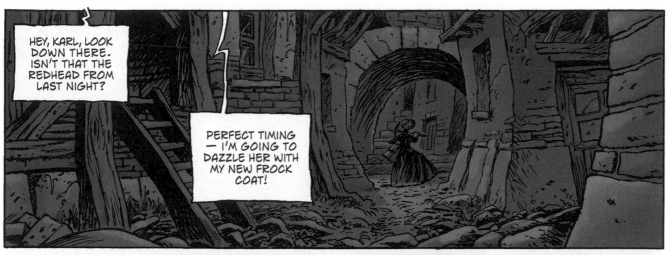

HEY, KARL, LOOK DOWN THERE. ISN'T THAT THE REDHEAD FROM LAST NIGHT?

PERFECT TIMING — I'M GOING TO DAZZLE HER WITH MY NEW FROCK COAT!

WATCH HOW THIS LADIES' MAN WORKS, AND LEARN!

HUP!

AHEM ... PRINCESS ...

?

LET ME INTRODUCE M'SELF: KARL HYDE ... ENTREPRENEUR ...

A PLEASURE, MR HYDE. I'M PRUDENCE. PRUDENCE ENDICOTT.

DO FORGIVE ME, THOUGH, BUT IT'S LATE AND I HAVE TO GO TO WORK!

29

I SHOULD HAVE PLACED A WAGER!

DIDN'T YOU SEE THAT SMOULDERING LOOK SHE GAVE ME?

UH, NO, I DIDN'T S—

OF COURSE YOU DIDN'T — YOU WERE TOO FAR! COME ON!!

MISS PRUDENCE! WAIT FOR US! ... YOU'LL PROBABLY NEED HARDY MEN TO HELP WITH YOUR WORK!

MRS PARKS? IT'S MISS ENDICOTT. LET ME IN!

KNOCK KNOCK KNOCK KNOCK

YOU ACTUALLY WOKE ME THIS TIME ... I'VE GOT USED TO THE SCRATCHING ...

SCRAT SCRAT SCRAT SC

GOOD EVENING, MRS PARKS! ...

?

I'M KARL HYDE, AND THIS IS DARREN. WE'RE MISS ENDICOTT'S ... PARTNERS!

SHHHH ...

I KNEW IT ... IT'S COMING FROM BELOW!

GENTLEMEN, YOU'RE GOING TO MOVE THIS WARDROBE!

30

DARREN! YOU LAZY BUM!! ... GNNNN! HELP ME, WILL YOU?!

MMF ... I'M HOLDING THE WHOLE THING!!

COULD YOU KEEP THE NOISE DOWN A LITTLE? ... MY HUSBAND IS ASLEEP UPSTAIRS AND HE GETS UP EARLY TOMORROW!

EXCELLENT! YOU CAN PUT IT DOWN NOW.

NOW WE NEED TO REMOVE THE FLOORBOARDS, RIGHT HERE!!

REMOVE THE FLOOR-BOARDS?! BUT ... WHY?

IT HAS TO BE DONE, YOU KNOW ... TO SOLVE YOUR PROBLEM.

WELL! IF IT HAS TO BE DONE ... DARREN!

WHACK WHACK WHACK

WHACK WHACK

THAT'LL DO, DARREN! ...

COUGH COUGH

MR HYDE, PLEASE BRING ME THE LAMP THAT'S INSIDE MY BAG.

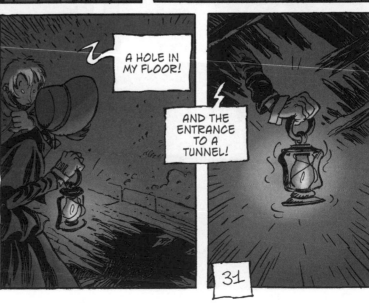

A HOLE IN MY FLOOR!

AND THE ENTRANCE TO A TUNNEL!

31

33

BETTER I SHOULD GO ALONE — IT COULD BE DANGEROUS!

DANGEROUS?

DANGER DOES NOT FRIGHTEN US, MISS PRUDENCE. IT'S ALL IN A DAY'S WORK FOR US!

DON'T BOTHER ...

SHE'S GONE DOWN THE HOLE ALREADY!

OH! MY HUSBAND'S AWAKE ...

I'M SURE HE'LL BE VERY GRATEFUL FOR ALL YOUR HELP.

GIMME THAT PICK-AXE, YOU!

WHAT'S GOING ON DOWN THERE?

ARE YOU THE ONE WHO MADE SUCH A MESS?

I DID, INDEED, ASSIST MISS ENDICOTT IN REARRANGING YOUR INTERIOR.

SBAM

32

34

HELLO,
MR SCRATCHER?

YOOHOO ...

MY EXIT
...

AH,
THERE
YOU ARE!

... THEY
STOLE MY
EXIT.

GOODNESS
ME! WHO
COULD HAVE
DONE SUCH
A THING?

THE NEW
PEOPLE ABOVE
... I SCRATCH
AND I SCRATCH,
BUT IT'S NO USE!

BACK WHEN IT WAS THE
THORNES, THERE WERE NO
PROBLEMS. I COULD GO FOR
A JAUNT ON THE SURFACE ...

... I'D GO
ABOUT MY
BUSINESS,
NICE AND
QUIET ...

... BUT NOW
I'M STUCK DOWN
HERE!

WE'LL FIND A
SOLUTION. THAT'S
WHAT I'M HERE FOR!

33

IS THAT ... TRUE? OH, MISS, THAT IS GOOD NEWS!

I'LL TALK TO THE PARKSES. I DON'T THINK THEY'LL OBJECT!

SEE THE LIGHTS FROM THE CITY OVER THERE? THAT'S MY HOME ...

WHERE DO YOU COME FROM, ANYWAY?

... OUR HOME. THE FORGOTTEN, THE WRETCHED, THE MISSHAPEN, THOSE THE PEOPLE ABOVE DON'T WANT TO SEE AND ONLY TOLERATE AT NIGHT, WHEN THE SHADOWS HIDE US.

AND THERE'S NO ONE TO HELP WHEN YOU'RE IN TROUBLE?

EH, NO. WE MAKE DO.

WELL, THAT IS GOING TO CHANGE!

PLEASE FOLLOW ME!

34

LET ME SEE IF I GOT THIS RIGHT: YOU WANT THAT MIDGET TO BE ABLE TO COME IN AND OUT OF MY HOUSE AT NIGHT AS HE PLEASES!

CORRECT!

OH, PLEASE! ... I WILL BE THE SOUL OF DISCRETION.

AND WHY SHOULD I AGREE TO IT?

TO BE NICE TO ME.

HMMM ...

COME ON, HENRY. HE LOOKS SO HARMLESS ... AND IF IT'LL LET US GET A GOOD NIGHT'S SLEEP ...

HMM ... ALL RIGHT, THEN. BUT HE'D BETTER NOT MESS UP THIS PLACE!

I PROMISE!

THERE YOU GO. MISSION ACCOMPLISHED!

THANK YOU, MISS ENDICOTT. I OWE YOU A GREAT DEBT!

I'LL SEE YOU ALL SOON.

35

THERE'S A MONSTER LIVING UNDER OUR HOUSE ... BUT IT'S ALL RIGHT.

LET'S GO TO BED.

BY THE WAY, WHAT HAPPENED TO THE TWO GENTLEMEN WHO CAME WITH ME?

THEY HAD TO LEAVE IN A HURRY ... ONE OF THEM WAS HAVING TROUBLE WITH HIS COAT ...

MY FROCK COAT ... MY TEETH ...

MY BACK ... LOSSES WERE HEAVY!

NEXT TIME YOU GO A-FLIRTING, I'M NOT COMING WITH YOU!

GRANTED, THE TASK MAY SEEM DAUNTING ...

... BUT I'M NOT GIVING UP SO EASILY ...

... PRUDENCE, ONE DAY YOU SHALL BE MINE!

36

THE PROBLEM IS SOLVED.

NOT BAD FOR A NOVICE. I TRUST IT WASN'T OVERLY DIFFICULT?

NOT AT ALL. HOWEVER, THE RESOLUTION IMPOSES A CERTAIN EVOLUTION!

OPEN THE WINDOWS — THIS MIGHT GET A LITTLE DUSTY ...

CRACK

YOU ARE CRAZY!!

I WANT TO BE EVERYONE'S CONCILIATOR! ...

... EVEN THE FORGOTTEN'S!

MARGUERITE MUST BE SPINNING IN HER GRAVE.

NEW CONCILIATOR ...

... NEW HABITS. SO YOU TOLD ME ALREADY.

37

I HAVE AN EXIT ... I HAVE AN EXIT ...

UGLY ... UGLY ... UGLY ...

YOU'RE A REBEL, SO YOU ARE ... THE REAL THING!

WE TELL YOU SOMETHING IMPORTANT, WE EXPLAIN IT FOR A LONG TIME SO YOU UNDERSTAND ... BUT YOU JUST WON'T LISTEN!

WH ... WHY DO YOU SAY THAT, ROCCO?

THE MASTER TOLD US NOT TO GO OUT AGAIN. NOT UNTIL THE BIG DAY ... BUT YOU HAVE TO GO A-SCRATCHING AND TALK TO THE PEOPLE ABOVE GROUND ...

YOU REALLY, REALLY SHOULDN'T HAVE!!

YOU KNOW THE PRICE!

MERCY, ROCCO, I WON'T DO IT AGAIN!

MERCY!

38

HEAVENS! IT'S WAR!!

THE FRENCH ARE ATTACKING!!

KNOCK KNOCK

DON'T WORRY, PRUDENCE. IT'S JUST ME, CONRAD ...

IT'S TIME TO GET UP!

A NEW DAY IS STARTING.

ALREADY?!

HOW ON EARTH WAS MY MOTHER ABLE TO BE A CONCILIATOR BY NIGHT AND MIDWIFE BY DAY?

EASY. SHE WAS LIKE ME ...

... AN INSOMNIAC.

WHEN I WAS LITTLE, SHE'D CALL ME 'SLEEPY KITTEN'.

HMMM ...

YOU'VE JUST ENOUGH TIME TO FRESHEN UP AND HAVE A CUP OF TEA!

39

YOU DON'T SLEEP WELL IN OUR HOUSE?

I DON'T SLEEP ENOUGH!

OH, FINALLY!

GOOD MORNING, EVAN ...

HEH. MAYBE I'LL GET USED TO IT IN TIME ...

... ALTHOUGH ...

HEY!

LOOK OUT!

HO-O

EEEEE EE

WHAT'S THE IDEA, CROSSING LIKE THAT WITHOUT LOOKING?! ...

I ALMOST ...

YOU!

YOU KNOW HIM?

BARELY.

I'M TRULY SORRY, MR PARKS. GOODBYE ...

COME ON, EVAN!

HEY! WHILE YOU'RE HERE ... LAST NIGHT YOU ASKED ME TO LET YOUR MIDGET COME THROUGH WHENEVER HE WANTED ...

... BUT THIS MORNING HIS HOLE WAS COMPLETELY FILLED IN ... MY FLOORBOARDS ARE INTACT — LIKE NEW ... WHAT WAS THE POINT OF WAKING ME UP?!

?

CAN WE KEEP GOING NOW? I'M IN A HURRY!!

OF COURSE. MY APOLOGIES.

IS THERE SOMETHING YOU'D LIKE TO ASK ME, EVAN?

ME? NO-O-O-O-O!

GOOD! LET'S GO AND GET SOME WAFFLES!

41

SAY, WOULD YOU LIKE ME TO READ YOU THE LETTER FROM MY PARENTS THAT CONRAD GAVE ME THIS MORNING?

IF YOU WANT.

HRMM ... DEAR EVAN ... WE'VE ARRIVED ON THE CONTINENT SAFELY ...

... WE MISS YOU VERY MUCH, BUT I'M SURE YOU UNDERSTAND THAT WE MUST DO EVERYTHING WE CAN TO FIND GRANDPA ...

... I HOPE YOU'RE GETTING ALONG WELL WITH YOUR NEW NANNY. SHE CAME WITH GLOWING RECOMMENDATIONS ...

... DON'T DRIVE HER TO DISTRACTION, AND STUDY HARD ... AS SOON AS WE'VE FOUND YOUR GRAND-FATHER, WE'LL COME BACK ...

... KNOW THAT YOU ARE IN OUR HEARTS ... YOUR LOVING PARENTS.

ARE YOU ALL RIGHT?

YES, YES ...

IT'S JUST THAT ... THEY'VE BEEN LOOKING FOR HIM FOR SO LONG ... I DON'T KNOW IF THEY'LL EVER FIND HIM.

42

LET'S GO AND LOOK AT SOME MATHEMATICS PROBLEMS. IT'LL TAKE YOUR MIND OFF THINGS.

IF YOU WANT!

... EVERYONE TALKS ABOUT THEM, THOUGH FEW HAVE SEEN THEM. YET, THEY EXIST!

COME, COME, LADIES AND GENTLEMEN! ...

?

THE HIPPOPOTAMUS MAN, THE WOMAN WITH 100 TEETH, THE HYDROCEPHALIC SIAMESE TWIN SISTERS ...

... FREAKS ARE AMONG US!

SHOULD WE GO AND SEE, MISS ENDICOTT?

I RATHER DOUBT THIS IS A SUITABLE SPECTACLE FOR YOU ... OR ANYONE ELSE, FOR THAT MATTER!

I SEE THAT SOME OF YOU ARE HESITATING. PERHAPS THEY THINK I'M TAKING THEM FOR FOOLS ... THAT I'M A CHARLATAN ...

I HAVE AN AMUSE-BOUCHE FOR SUCH PEOPLE ... ONE OF THE FINEST PIECES IN MY COLLECTION ...

... LADIES AND GENTLEMEN, BEHOLD ...

IGOR! ... ... THE HORRIBLE MOUSTACHIOED DWARF!!

43

HAVE YOU SEEN HOW GROTESQUE HE IS?

HE'S NOT THE ONLY ONE!

I WANT TO SEE THE REST ... THE OTHER FREAKS!

I DON'T THINK SO! ... AS LONG AS I'M YOUR NANNY, AT ANY RATE, YOU MOST CERTAINLY WILL NOT!

TIME TO GO HOME.

SOMETIMES I DON'T UNDERSTAND YOU, MISS ENDICOTT.

SO, I HAVE TO CALCULATE HOW MANY FLOORBOARDS TO REMOVE IN ORDER TO MAKE A HOLE THAT'S 20 FEET SQUARE?

I REALLY WONDER WHERE YOU GET THE IDEAS FOR YOUR EXERCISES.

WELL, I GUESS I'LL FIGURE IT OUT ON MY OWN.

44

COMING THROUGH!

?

HERE'S SOMETHING THAT SHOULD PUT A SMILE ON YOUR FACE!

MISS ENDICOTT! **WELSH RAREBIT!!**

YOU WORKED HARD TODAY. YOU'VE EARNED A REWARD!

YUM!

MMM ... THE HEAVENLY SMELL OF CHEDDAR!

CRUNCH GLP ...

I'LL NEED YOU TO GO UP TO YOUR ROOM IMMEDIATELY AFTER DINNER, EVAN. I HAVE TO GO OUT AGAIN TONIGHT.

OH, THAT'S ALL RIGHT. AFTER SUCH A FEAST, I'LL SLEEP LIKE A LOG!

GOOD NIGHT, MISS ENDICOTT.

SLURP!

GOOD NIGHT, EVAN.

45

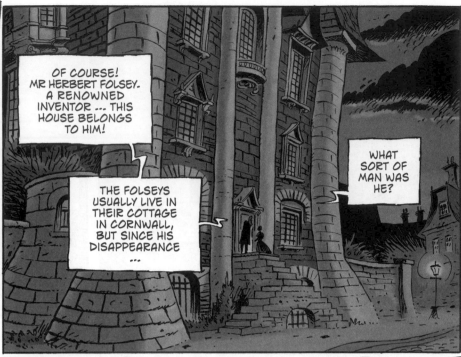

EVAN SEEMS RATHER VULNERABLE, WHAT WITH HIS PARENTS AWAY AND HIS GRANDFATHER MISSING.

OF COURSE! MR HERBERT FOLSEY. A RENOWNED INVENTOR ... THIS HOUSE BELONGS TO HIM!

WHAT SORT OF MAN WAS HE?

OH ... HE TOLD YOU ABOUT HIM?

VAGUELY, THIS MORNING ... DID YOU KNOW HIM?

THE FOLSEYS USUALLY LIVE IN THEIR COTTAGE IN CORNWALL, BUT SINCE HIS DISAPPEARANCE ...

AN ECCENTRIC ONE!

ALWAYS HUNGRY FOR NEW THRILLS. HE LEFT TO EXPLORE THE WORLD ...

... APPARENTLY, DURING HIS TRAVELS HE FOUND A MAGNIFICENT PLACE — A TRUE ELDORADO, UNDISCOVERED BY MAN ...

... WHEN HE RETURNED, HE WASN'T THE SAME. ALL HE WANTED WAS TO GO BACK THERE AND STAY FOR EVER ...

... THEN, ONE DAY, HE VANISHED WITHOUT A TRACE ...

... THE FOLSEYS ARE CONVINCED HE'S LOST HIS MIND AND IS IN GREAT DANGER, WHICH IS WHY THEY LEFT TO LOOK FOR HIM SO HURRIEDLY!

THAT SOUNDS ALMOST LIKE A MISSION FOR A CONCILIATOR.

ALAS, YOU DON'T HAVE TIME TO TRAVEL THE WORLD!

NO, I DON'T HAVE THE TIME ANY MORE.

46

OH, DID YOU THROW AWAY THE DINNER SIMONE PREPARED? DISCREETLY?

DON'T WORRY. THERE IS NO WAY SHE COULD SUSPECT A THING.

EXCELLENT!

NO ONE! ... YET, I COULD HAVE SWORN ...

... LET'S PUT IT DOWN TO LACK OF SLEEP.

FINALLY I'M GOING TO FIND OUT YOUR SE—

SO, THIS IS WHERE YOU SPEND YOUR NIGHTS, MISS ENDICOTT ...

HMMF ...

48

THREE DAYS. CAN YOU BELIEVE IT? ... SHE'S ONLY BEEN HERE THREE DAYS, I HAVEN'T EVEN MET HER YET, AND ALREADY SHE'S MAKING LIFE IMPOSSIBLE FOR ME ...

THE CONCILIATOR HAS ARRIVED ...

OH! GOOD!

?

HOW CAN I BE OF HELP, MS ... ?

BEAUREGARD! ...

... SIMONE BEAUREGARD ...

I WORK AS A GOURMET CHEF IN A LARGE TOWNHOUSE ... FOR THE LAST FEW DAYS, THOUGH, SOMEONE HAS BEEN INTERFERING WITH MY COOKING ...

I STILL ONLY KNOW HER BY NAME, BUT I ALREADY LOATHE THIS ...

... PRUDENCE ENDICOTT!

THE NEW NANNY. SHE IS BRINGING MY TALENT FOR GASTRONOMY INTO DISREPUTE. SHE HAS THE GALL TO THROW MY DISHES OUT THE WINDOW AND SNEAKILY FEED MY EMPLOYERS' SON WITH DUBIOUS COMESTIBLES ...

SHE MADE YOUNG MASTER EVAN FORCE DOWN HER REVOLTING CONCOCTION WHILE LISTENING TO QUESTIONABLE MUSIC!

MY WORD! THIS IS SERIOUS! ... WHAT ARE YOU LOOKING FOR, MS BEAUREGARD?

I'D LIKE YOU TO CONVINCE HER TO CHANGE HER ATTITUDE ... CRUNCH ...

HMM ... YOUR BISCUITS ARE DELICIOUS!

OF COURSE, THE BEST OUTCOME WOULD BE FOR HER TO LEAVE HER POSITION IN MY HOUSEHOLD.

INDEED!

I'LL SEE WHAT I CAN DO ... THOUGH I CANNOT PROMISE THE IMPOSSIBLE!

49

WHEN DO YOU THINK YOU'LL BE ABLE TO REPORT TO ME ABOUT YOUR INVESTIGATION?

SOONER THAN YOU THINK!

WELL, THEN I WILL S—

HEAVENS! WHAT IS THAT?!

EEEEEEEE!

EEEEEEEEEEEEEEEEE EEEEEEEEEE

WELL, NOW! THIS IS NEW!

HE LOOKS ...

... YES! THAT'S THE POOR MAN FROM LAST NIGHT!

HE'S IN A BAD WAY!

HE'S GOING TO STAIN MY FLOOR.

WE NEED TO SEE TO HIS WOUNDS RIGHT AWAY. BOIL SOME WATER!

50

DID YOU EVEN NOTICE THE WORK I DID ON THE ACCESS HOLE?

I NOTICED.

WE ARE NOW CONNECTED TO A NETWORK OF TUNNELS THAT RUN BENEATH THE WHOLE CITY ...

... SOMETHING I LEARNT FROM THAT BOOK YOU WERE READING THE OTHER NIGHT.

HENCEFORTH, THE DREGS OF HUMANITY SHALL END UP IN OUR PARLOUR!

HUSH — I THINK. HE'S TRYING TO SAY SOMETHING.

'IT HURTS'?

SHHH!

M ... MISS ENDICOTT ...

AT LEAST HE KNOWS YOUR NAME!

HE PASSED OUT!

DON'T WORRY. HIS INJURIES ARE NOT FATAL. HE'S MERELY EXHAUSTED.

YOU THINK SO?

DO TRUST ME, MISS PRUDENCE. FOR A CHANGE.

51

I MUST FIND OUT WHAT HAPPENED!

DON'T YOU HAVE ANOTHER CASE PENDING?

YOU'RE JOKING, I HOPE?

SIMONE APPEARED QUITE DETERMINED IN HER PETITION.

SIMONE CAN WAIT. I'M GOING FOR A WALK!

DO, DO.

LOOK AFTER THE WOUNDED FELLOW WHILE I'M GONE. I'LL QUESTION HIM WHEN I RETURN.

IF YOU RETURN!

OH, DON'T YOU WORRY — I WILL RETURN!

MISS MARGUERITE USED TO SAY THE SAME THING!

52

54

THE CITY OF THE FORGOTTEN.

IT LOOKS ENORMOUS!

IT'S INCREDIBLE. HOW CAN NO ONE HAVE NOTICED IT BEFORE?

THE STREETS AREN'T EXACTLY THRONGED ...

UH-HUM ...

53

OH! SOMEONE AT LAST! GOOD EVENING, MR ... ?

MISTER? ... NOW, THAT'S FUNNY ... NO ONE'S EVER CALLED ME MISTER. I'M DOUGIE, HIGH ELDER OF THE CITY ...

... BUT I LIKE THE SOUND OF MR DOUGIE. FROM NOW ON, YOU'LL HAVE TO CALL ME THAT.

A PLEASURE, MR DOUGIE. I'M PRUDENCE.

I SUPPOSE THE MASTER SENT YOU?

YES ... OF COURSE ... I WOULD NEVER HAVE COME ON MY OWN.

I HOPE THE MASTER ISN'T LOSING PATIENCE — EVERYTHING WILL BE READY SOON!

SCRAT SCRAT

REALLY?

IT'S TRUE THAT WE'VE FALLEN BEHIND ON THE MACHINE'S CONSTRUCTION, BUT TOMORROW AT MIDNIGHT, IT CAN BE TURNED ON.

IT'LL BE GLORIOUS! AN ABSOLUTE REVOLUTION!

REVOLUTION!

REVOLUTION!

REVOLUTION!

GOOD, GOOD! ... SO, UH ... I'D LIKE TO SEE THE FAMOUS MACHINE!

54

OF COURSE, OF COURSE ...

IT'S THAT WAY!

OH! A LADY FROM ABOVE!

SHE'S SO PRETTY!

SUCH FINE CLOTHES!

HER SKIN ...

LOVELY GLOVES ... MAY I HAVE ONE?

LEAVE THE LADY ALONE ... SHE WAS SENT BY THE MASTER!

OHHHHH !!!

THE MASTER!

THE LIBERATOR!

THE ONLY ONE TO TAKE CARE OF US AT LAST.

GOOD MASTER!

PLEASE THANK HIM FOR WHAT HE'S ABOUT TO ACCOMPLISH!

FORGIVE THEM — THEY HAVE NO MANNERS!

IT'S ALL RIGHT. I UNDERSTAND.

SO, THIS MACHINE? ...

PATIENCE! WE'RE ALMOST THERE.

THERE IT IS! QUITE THE THING, ISN'T IT? ... A REVOLUTION, AS I TOLD YOU!

55

THE MASTER TOLD ME LITTLE ABOUT ITS FUNCTION.

REVOLUTION!

REVOLUTION!

THAT'S STRANGE ... I THOUGHT YOU WERE HERE TO CONFIRM THAT IT WOULD WORK ...

UH ... YES, AND MORE.

ARE YOU SURE YOU WERE SENT BY THE MASTER?

WHY, YES, OBVIOUSLY!

YOU COULD HAVE FOLLOWED ONE OF THE TUNNELS LEADING TO THE SURFACE ... BUT ALL OF THEM WERE BLOCKED LONG AGO.

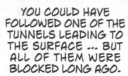

TO BE HONEST, ACTUALLY, I'M HERE TO INVESTIGATE AN ATTACK ON AN ACQUAINTANCE.

OHHHH!

LIES!

LIES!

LIES!

YOU SHOULDN'T HAVE COME ... YOU SHOULDN'T HAVE ...

THE MASTER WON'T BE PLEASED ... HE WON'T BE!!

NO, WAIT! DON'T GO!

PRUDENCE, YOU'RE BETTER AT LYING TO COOKS THAN TO OLD MEN IN THEIR FINERY!

WELL, SINCE I'M HERE ...

56

IT LOOKS LIKE ONE OF THOSE REVOLUTIONARY NEW MACHINES THEY SHOWED AT THE LAST WORLD EXPOSITION ...

... A GIGANTIC STEAM ENGINE?

THE PIPES GO ALL THE WAY TO THE SURFACE!

WHAT'S GOING TO HAPPEN TOMORROW AT MIDNIGHT?

YOU'LL KNOW SOON ENOUGH!

?

BUT FOR NOW, YOU DON'T BELONG HERE, SLYBOOTS.

WHO ON EARTH TAUGHT YOU YOUR MANNERS? THIS IS NO WAY TO ADDRESS A LADY!

YOU'RE RIGHT ABOUT THAT ...

... BUT THEN, THIS IS NO PLACE FOR A LADY!

57

YOU'RE FAR, SO FAR FROM THE SURFACE!

I WAS TAKING A WALK!

DON'T LIE! YOU'RE SPYING ON US!

I'M INVESTIGATING ...

YOU CONFESS QUICKLY! ... IT'S DANGEROUS TO COME NOSING ABOUT THIS PLACE ...

IS THAT A THREAT?

THERE ARE RULES, AND MY COMPANIONS AND I ARE TASKED WITH MAKING SURE THEY ARE FOLLOWED!

RULES WRITTEN BY THE MASTER?

THAT DOESN'T MATTER! ...

... YOU SHOULDN'T HAVE COME HERE. OTHERS BEFORE YOU BROKE THE RULES ... THEY PAID THE PRICE!!

LIKE THE POOR LITTLE MAN WHO CRAWLED TO MY OFFICE TO FIND HELP!

58

DO YOU MEAN UGLY JOE, BY ANY CHANCE? ... A FOOL WHO WANTED TO LEAVE BEFORE THE BIG DAY.

YOU ... YOU'RE THE ONE WHO BEAT HIM SO BADLY!

I CALL IT A GOOD LESSON ... FINE WORK, I MUST SAY!

YOU'RE A MONSTER!

AND YOU A TYPICAL SURFACE DWELLER, JUDGING BY SOMEONE'S APPEARANCE ...

YOU'RE WRONG THERE ... CRUELTY HAS NO FACE!

YEAH, WELL, ENOUGH PREACHING! FOLLOW US NICELY TO YOUR CELL ... WE'LL LET YOU GO ONCE IT'S ALL OVER.

ABSOLUTELY NOT. I DO NOT ACKNOWLEDGE YOUR AUTHORITY!

AS YOU WISH, MISS ...

... YOU HAVE FUN, LADS!!

OH, DEAR. HOW ... FRIGHTENING ...

59

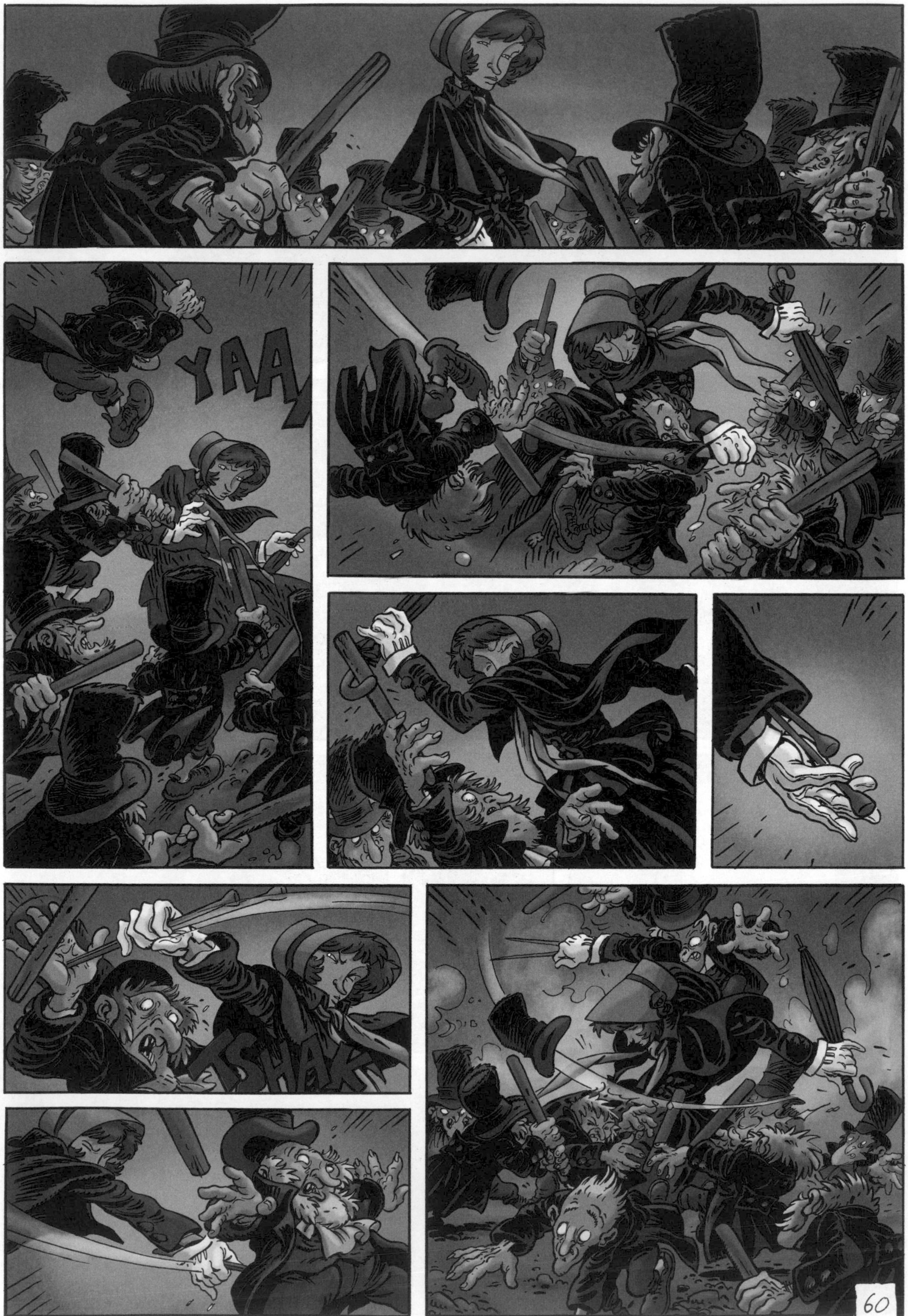
YAA
TSHAK
60

WELL, IT LOOKS LIKE IT'S JUST THE TWO OF US ONCE AGAIN.

IMPRESSIVE! ...

... BUT DON'T START CELEBRATING JUST YET! ... I STILL HAVE A LOT OF FRIENDS WHO DREAM OF MEETING YOU!

61

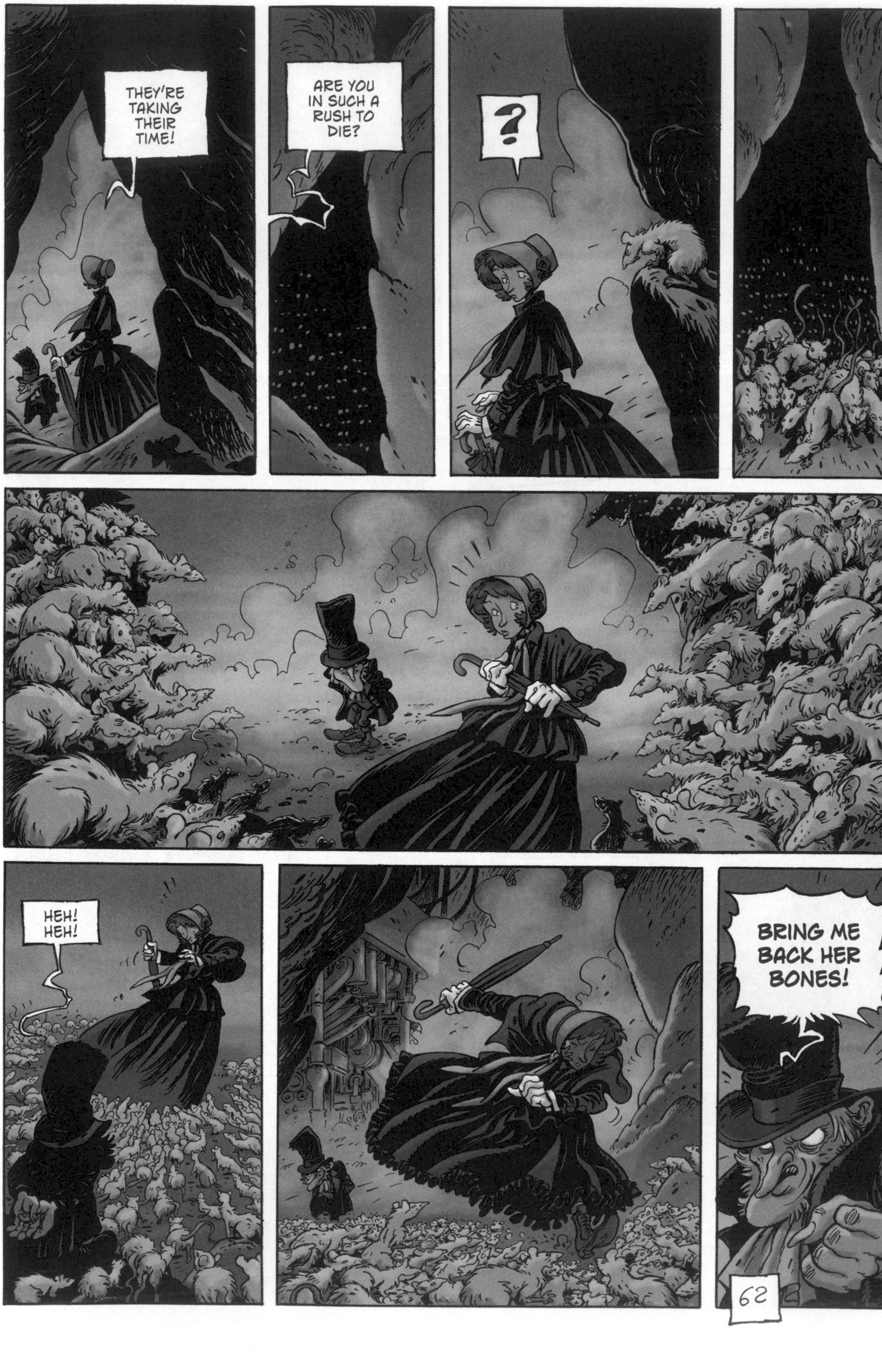
THEY'RE TAKING THEIR TIME!
ARE YOU IN SUCH A RUSH TO DIE?
?
HEH! HEH!
BRING ME BACK HER BONES!
62

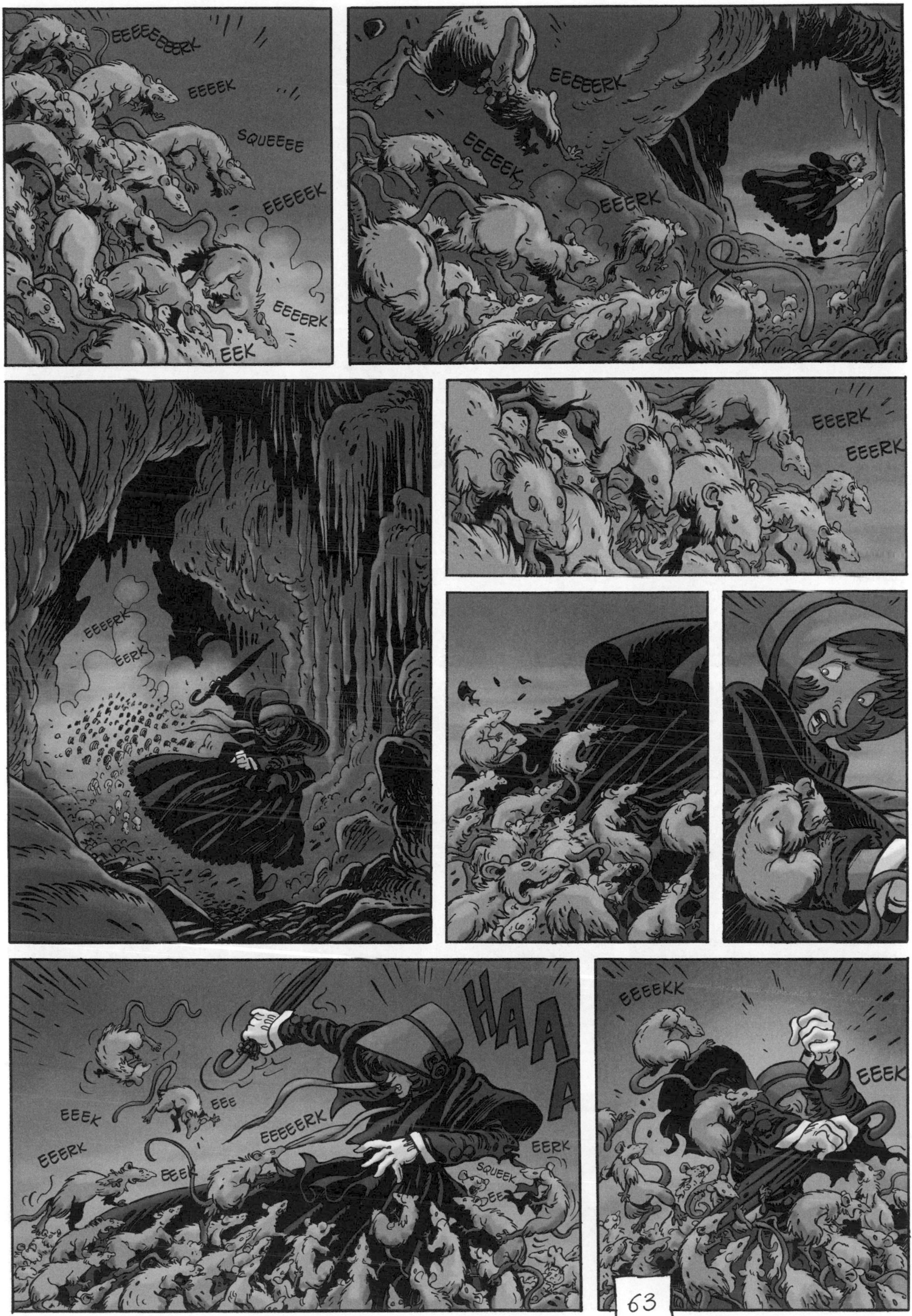
EEEEEEEEERK
EEEEK
SQUEEEE
EEEEEK
EEEERK
EEK
EEEEEERK
EEEEEK
EEERK
EEERK
EEERK
EEEERK
EEERK
HAAAA
EEEK
EEE
EEERK
EEEEERK
EEE
EERK
SQUEEK
EEE
EEEEKK
EEEK
63

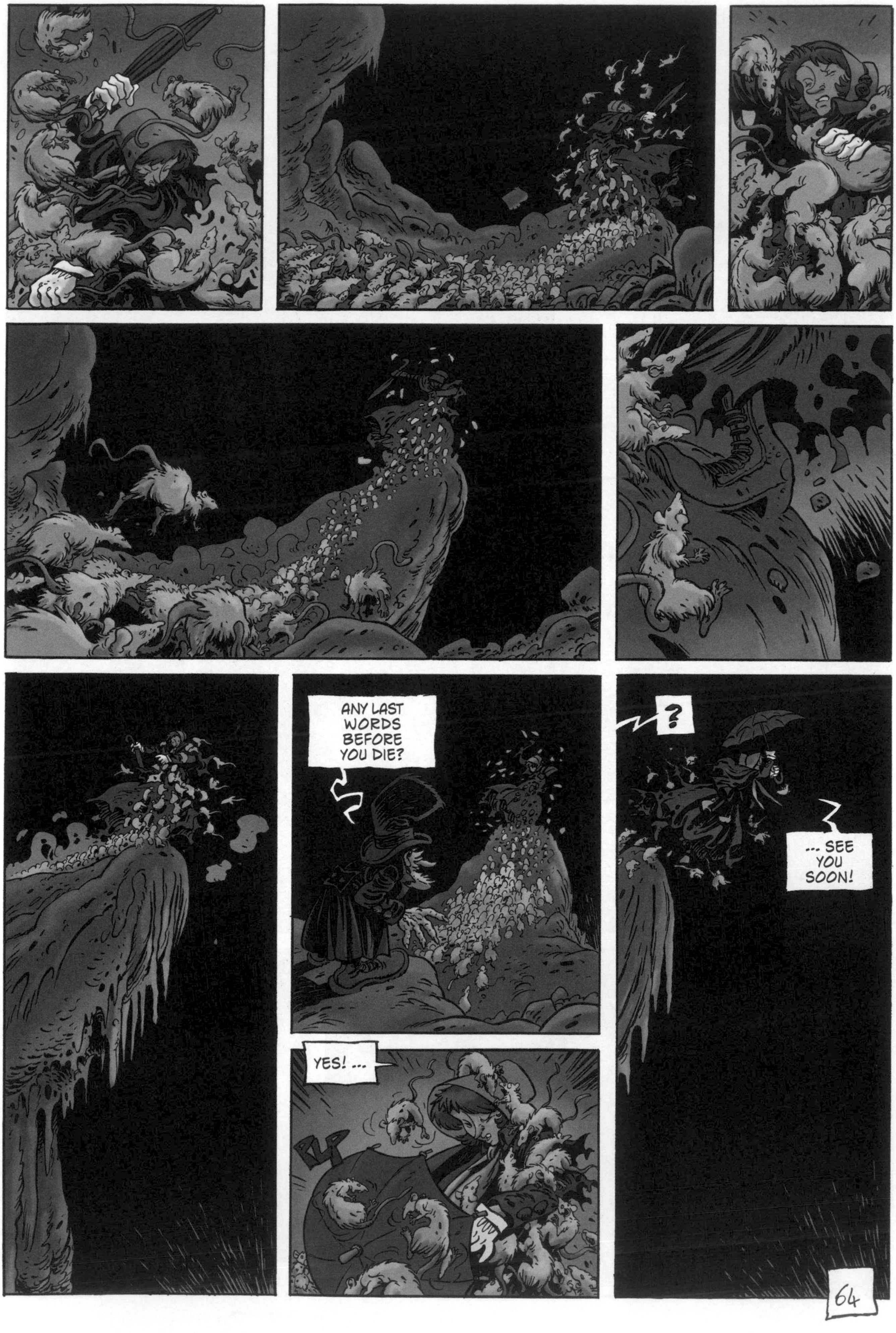
ANY LAST WORDS BEFORE YOU DIE?
?
... SEE YOU SOON!
YES! ...
64

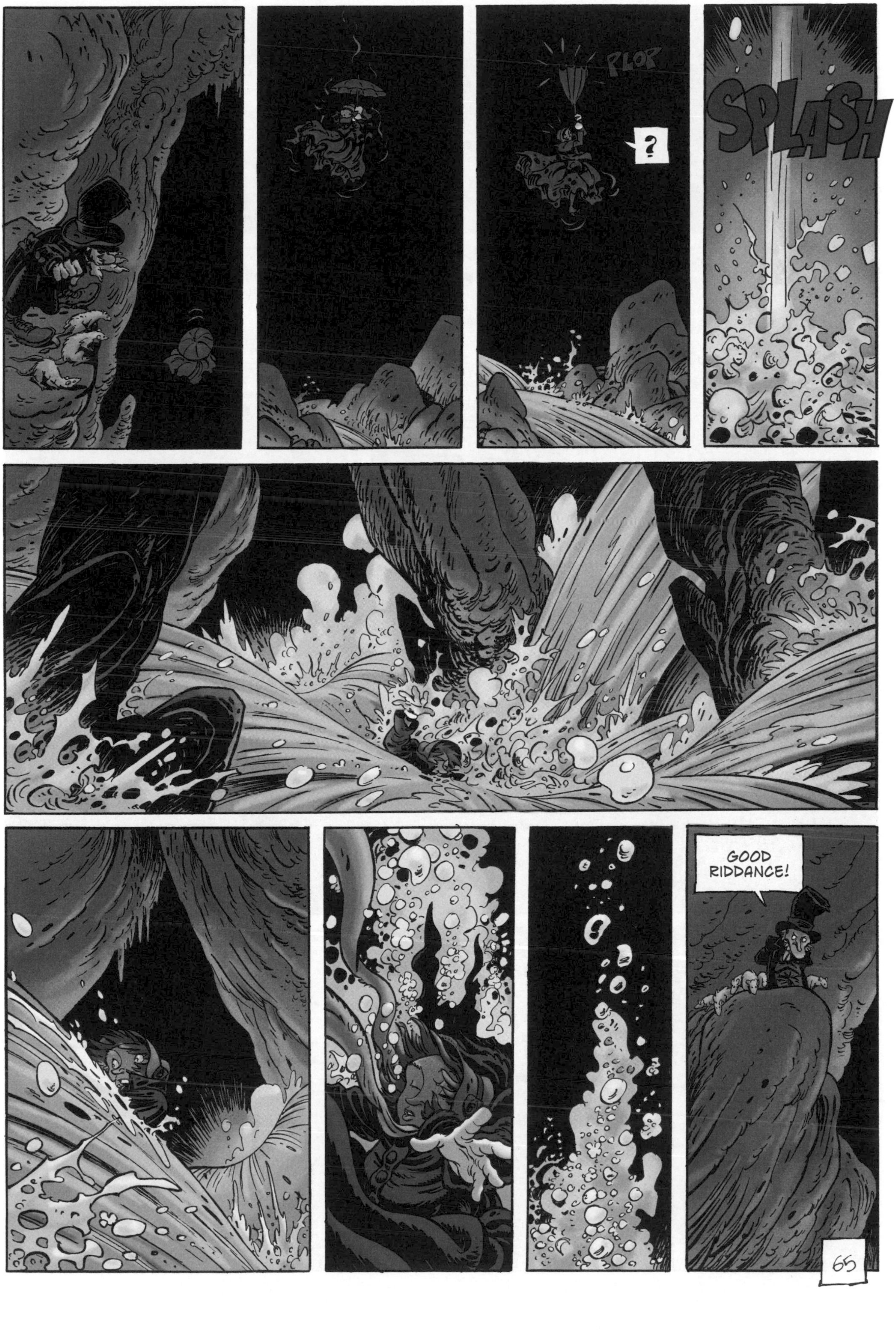
PLOP
?
SPLASH
GOOD RIDDANCE!
65

BLP
BLP

COUGH
COUGH

THE PARK ...

I'M IN THE PARK!

COUGH
COUGH

GROAAA

D'YOU REALLY THINK IT'S A GOOD IDEA TO STEAL THE ZOO'S LION?

IT'S NOT A GOOD IDEA, IT'S AN EXCELLENT IDEA. AS IT SHOULD BE, SINCE IT'S MINE!!

THOSE VOICES ... I KNOW THEM.

66

WE'LL BE RICH ONCE WE SELL THAT ANIMAL!

TO WHO?

BOY, YOU DO ASK STUPID QUESTIONS SOMETIMES ...

HA!

SO, LET'S REVIEW THE PLAN ... I OPEN THE CAGE ... AND YOU SUBDUE THE CREATURE AND—

SHH! SOMEONE'S COMING!

THAT'S NOT A GUARDIAN.

NO, I'D SAY MORE LIKE YOUR FUTURE FIANCÉE ... LOOKING HALF DEAD!

DON'T BE SILLY!

WELL, LOOK.

BLIMEY! PRUDENCE!

OH, NO! WHAT THE DEVIL HAPPENED TO HER?

SHE'S IN NO SHAPE TO TELL US.

TAKE ME BACK HOME ...

UH ... GLADLY, BUT WHERE'S HOME?

122 PHOENIX ROAD.

RIGHT! ... DARREN, HELP ME GET HER UP!!

67

LOOK AT THAT — I'M GETTING ALL DIRTY!

AS OPPOSED TO WHAT YOU CALL CLEAN?

YEAH, WELL, I'M NOT SURE I CAN CARRY HER ALL THE WAY TO HER PLACE.

QUIT COMPLAINING. EXERCISE IS GOOD FOR YOU.

SHE'S PROBABLY GOT MONEY. WE COULD TAKE A CARRIAGE.

NOT THE WORST IDEA! AND TIMELY — THERE'S ONE COMING!

HEY!

?

SORRY, I DON'T TAKE VAGR—

THEM!

HIM!

UH ... IT'S AN ABSOLUTE EMERGENCY. WE FOUND MISS ENDICOTT BY THE LAKE, FREEZING-LIKE ...

... WE'RE TAKING HER HOME.

HMM ...

ALL RIGHT, THEN ... FOR HER, THE FARE IS ON THE HOUSE. MIND YOU DON'T DIRTY EVERYTHING UP INSIDE, THOUGH!

68

DON'T WORRY, PRUDENCE. EVERYTHING WILL BE ALL RIGHT!

NOT IF HE KEEPS DRIVING SO FAST — I'M GOING TO BE SICK!

Z

WE'RE HERE!

ABOUT TIME ... BURP!

SO, THIS IS WHERE YOU LIVE.

THE LIGHT IS STILL ON.

OH, PRUDENCE! AT LAST!

CONRAD ... WHAT ARE YOU DOING UP AT THIS HOUR? ... DID SOMETHING HAPPEN?

IT'S EVAN ...

... HE'S GONE!

WHAT?!

EVAN? WHO'S EVAN?

HE'S LEFT THE HOUSE — THROUGH THE WINDOW.

HE MUST HAVE TRIED TO FOLLOW ME.

WHAT IF HE RAN INTO THE WRONG SORT?

I HAVE TO FIND HIM RIGHT AWAY! MR PARKS, PLEASE, CAN YOU TAKE ME TO MY OFFICE? THE SAFETY OF A YOUNG BOY IS AT STAKE!

I'M COMING WITH YOU!

SO ARE WE! GET IN, DARREN!

OH, NO ...

?

69

BIT OF A TIGHT FIT ... DARREN, YOU SHOULD HAVE WALKED.

I WISH I HAD! GULP ...

I CAN'T TAKE YOU ANY CLOSER — THE COACH WON'T FIT!

THAT'S FINE. THANKS, AGAIN!

THERE, LOOK!

THAT HAT ... THAT'S EVAN'S!

AND THIS CLOTH ...

CHLOROFORM ... HE WAS PUT TO SLEEP ... ABDUCTED?

MISS ENDICOTT!

70

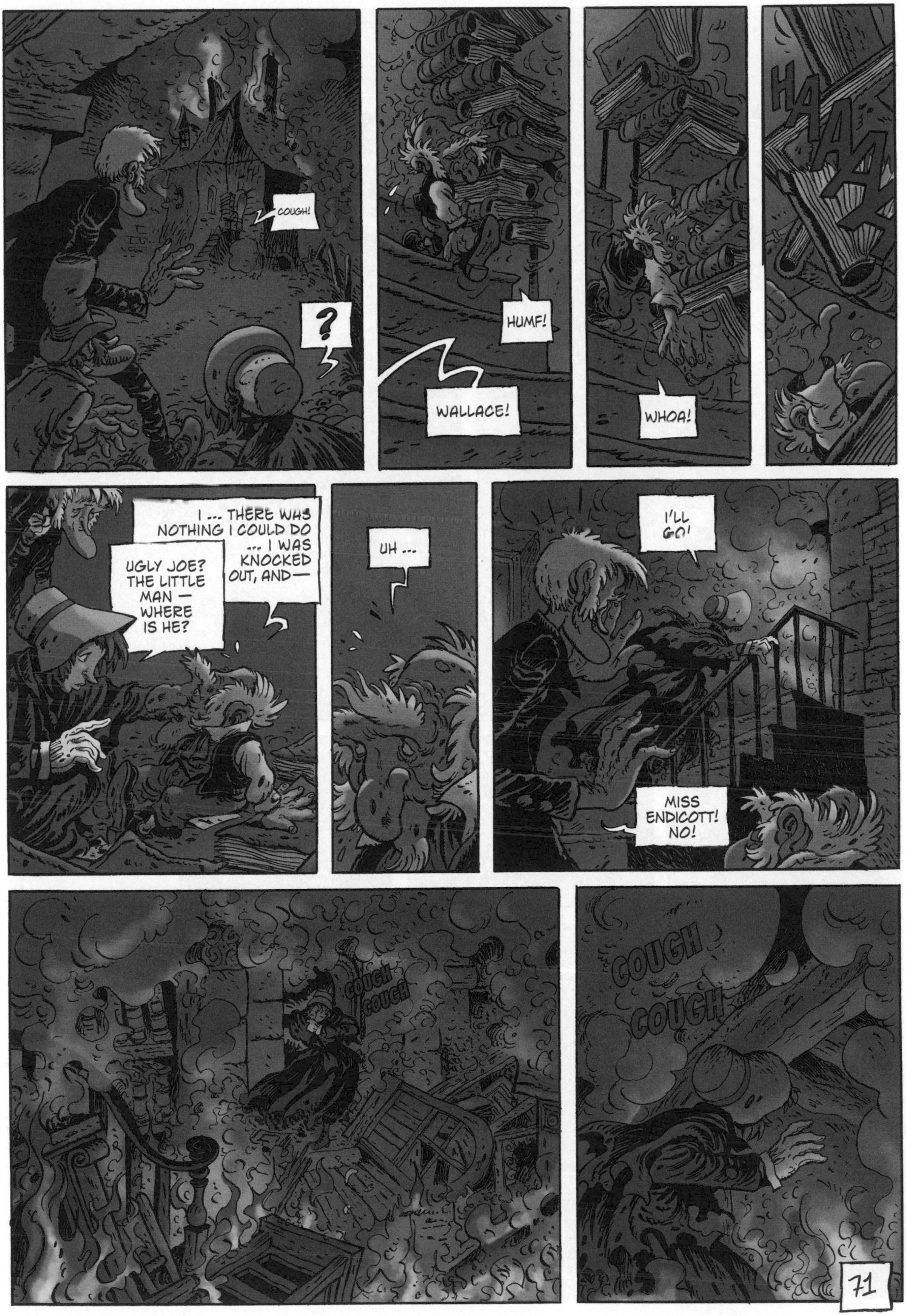
COUGH!
?
HUMF!
WALLACE!
WHOA!
HAAAA
I ... THERE WAS NOTHING I COULD DO ... I WAS KNOCKED OUT, AND—
UGLY JOE? THE LITTLE MAN — WHERE IS HE?
UH ...
I'LL GO!
MISS ENDICOTT! NO!
COUGH COUGH
COUGH COUGH
71

IT WOULD BE MADNESS — THE ROOF COULD COLLAPSE AT ANY SEC—

WE HAVE TO RESCUE HER!

KRRAAAAA A

THERE!

COUGH! ... I'M FINE. WE BOTH ARE ... HE'S STILL UNCONSCIOUS, BUT THE FLAMES DIDN'T REACH HIM.

THE CONCILIATORS' HOUSE ... GONE UP IN SMOKE ... SNIFF ...

72

THERE ... HE'LL BE SAFE HERE.

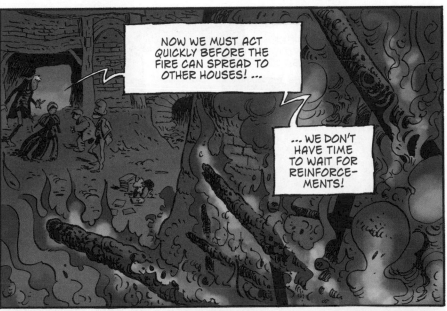

NOW WE MUST ACT QUICKLY BEFORE THE FIRE CAN SPREAD TO OTHER HOUSES! ...

... WE DON'T HAVE TIME TO WAIT FOR REINFORCE-MENTS!

GO AND GET SOME CONTAINERS! ... THERE'S A PUMP OVER THERE. WE'LL FORM A CHAIN!

?

WE?

I MEAN ... IT'S GETTING LATE ... AND WE WERE THINKING THAT, MAYBE ...

COME ON! COME ON!

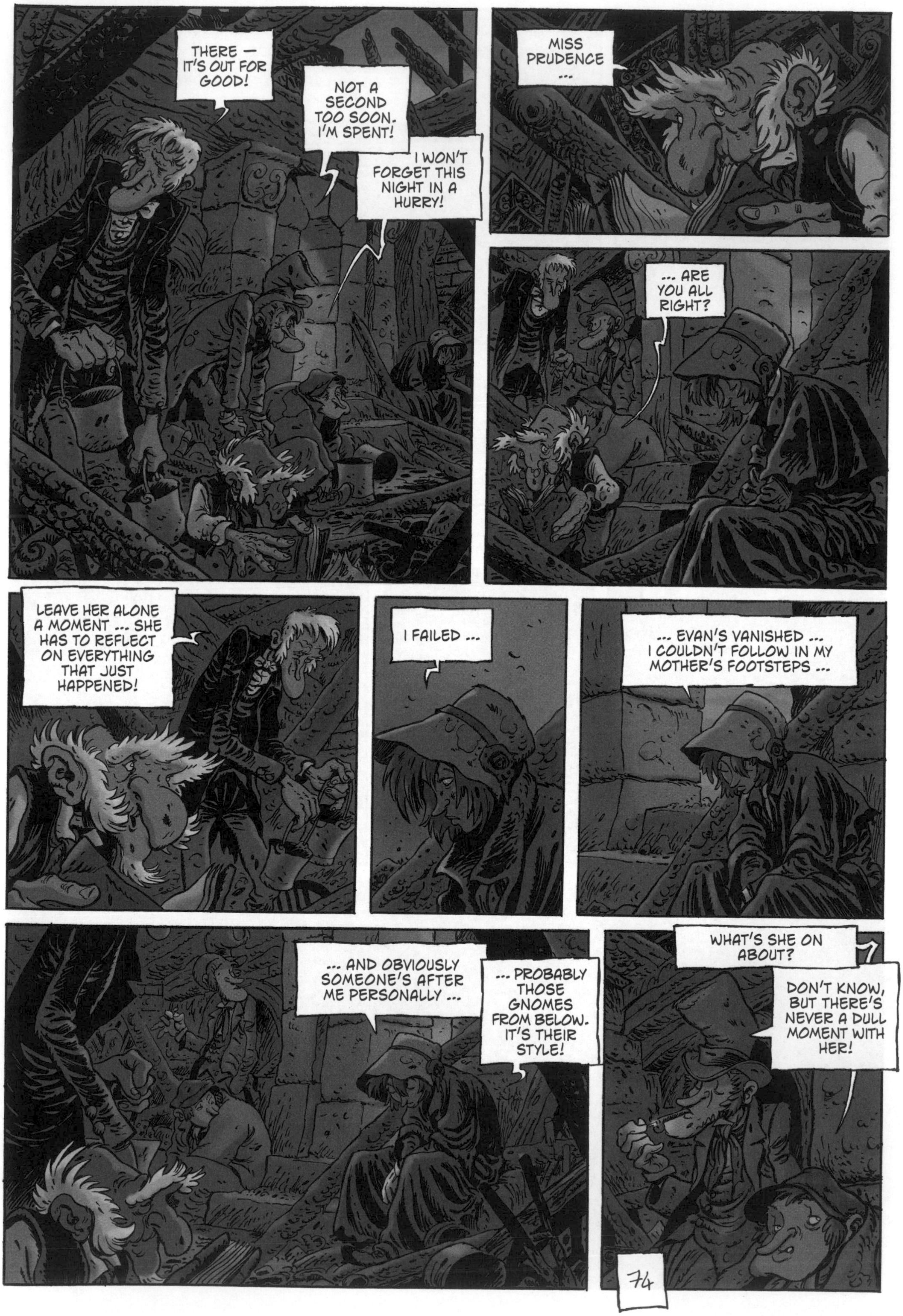
THERE — IT'S OUT FOR GOOD!
NOT A SECOND TOO SOON. I'M SPENT!
I WON'T FORGET THIS NIGHT IN A HURRY!
MISS PRUDENCE ...
... ARE YOU ALL RIGHT?
LEAVE HER ALONE A MOMENT ... SHE HAS TO REFLECT ON EVERYTHING THAT JUST HAPPENED!
I FAILED ...
... EVAN'S VANISHED ... I COULDN'T FOLLOW IN MY MOTHER'S FOOTSTEPS ...
... AND OBVIOUSLY SOMEONE'S AFTER ME PERSONALLY ...
... PROBABLY THOSE GNOMES FROM BELOW. IT'S THEIR STYLE!
WHAT'S SHE ON ABOUT?
DON'T KNOW, BUT THERE'S NEVER A DULL MOMENT WITH HER!
74

MISS ENDICOTT ... WE HAVE TO ALERT THE AUTHORITIES ... THE POLICE ... EVAN MUST BE FOUND WITHOUT DELAY!

YES!

IT'S WHAT MATTERS MOST. I DON'T WANT ANYTHING TO HAPPEN TO HIM BECAUSE OF ME! ...

I'M READY! ...

READY TO ACCEPT THE CONSEQUENCES OF MY ACTIONS!

YOU WON, MUM!

YOU KNEW I'D NEVER BE ABLE TO REPLACE YOU ...

... YOU TOLD ME SO WHEN I LEFT FOR INDIA!

WHO'S SHE TALKING TO?

75

SHE'S SOLILO-QUISING!

BLESS YOU!

BUT I WILL FIGHT — MAKE NO MISTAKE!

I WILL PROVE TO YOU THAT I CAN DO IT! ...

...AND NOTHING, NO ONE, WILL STOP ME!!

NO TIME FOR SLEEP, GENTLEMEN! WE MUST SUCCEED!

TIME TO SHOW OUR ENEMIES HOW A CONCILIATOR FIGHTS!

TONIGHT?

UH ...

?!

YEAAAAH!

WELL, I CAN'T WAIT TO SEE THAT!

76

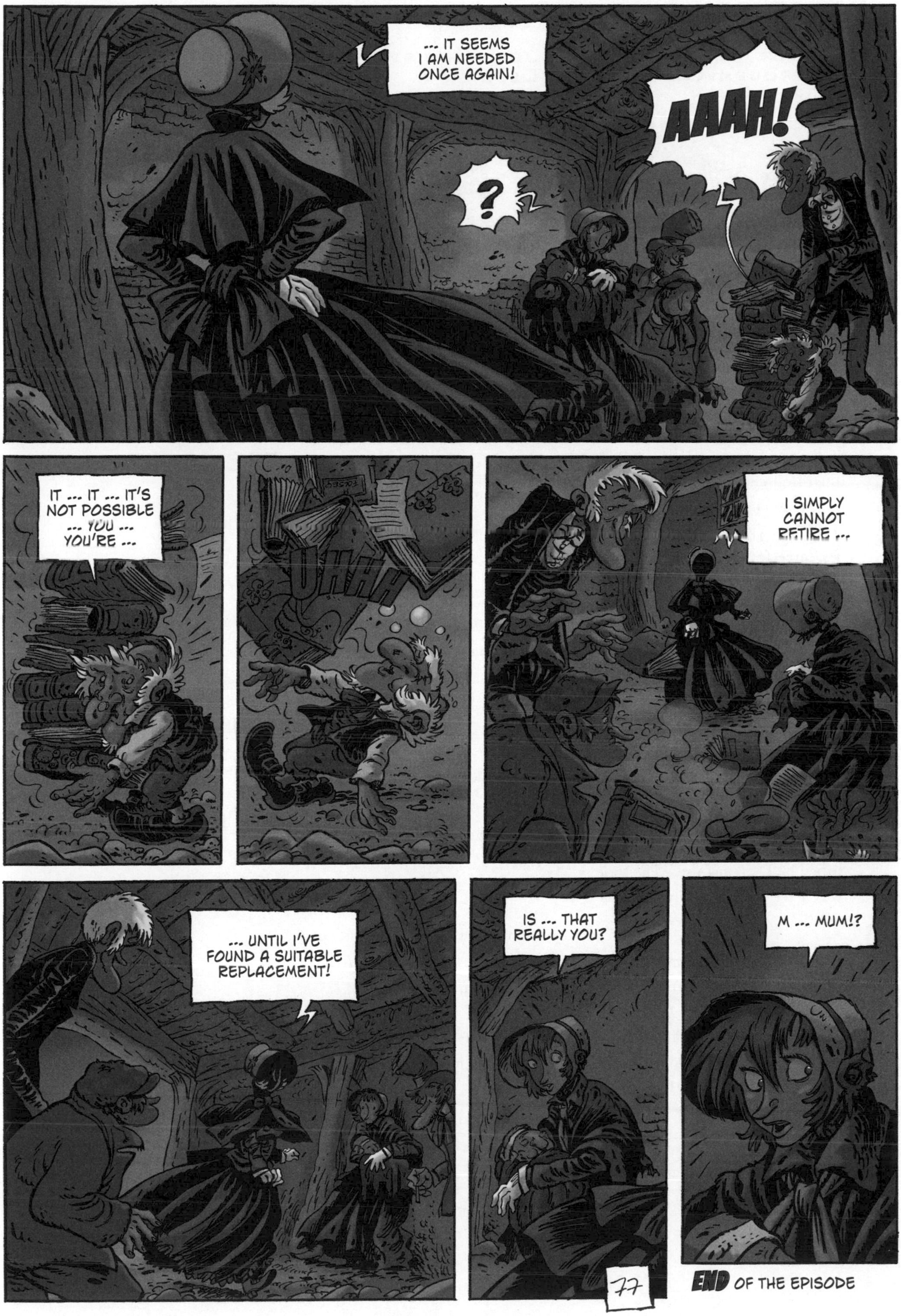
... IT SEEMS I AM NEEDED ONCE AGAIN!
?
AAAH!
IT ... IT ... IT'S NOT POSSIBLE ... YOU ... YOU'RE ...
UHHH
I SIMPLY CANNOT RETIRE ...
... UNTIL I'VE FOUND A SUITABLE REPLACEMENT!
IS ... THAT REALLY YOU?
M ... MUM!?
77

END OF THE EPISODE

XAVIER FOURQUEMIN
Artist

© C. de Torquat.

Born in Neuilly-sur-Seine in 1970. After going to school first in Bagneux, in the suburbs of Paris, then in Toulouse, Xavier Fourquemin graduated from high school in 1990. A few years later, he achieved a degree from the *bande dessinée* section of the Tournai Academy of Fine Arts in Belgium, after four years of study under Antonio Cossu.

In 1996 came his first publication: *L'immonde bête* (a story in four pages) in *Gotham* magazine (Vent d'Ouest). The following year saw the beginning of the prepublication of *Alban* in *Golem* magazine (Le Téméraire). Then, in January 1998, the first volume of *Alban* was published by Le Téméraire. (The series was later picked up by publisher Soleil.)

In January 2001, he began the series *Outlaw* (Glénat); then, from 2008 to 2012, he published *La Légende du Changeling* (Le Lombard), from a story steeped in folklore written by Pierre Dubois. Since 2012 he's been drawing *Le Train des Orphelins*, with Philippe Charlot (Bamboo), of which four volumes are out already.

JEAN-CHRISTOPHE DERRIEN
Writer

© C. de Torquat

Jean-Christophe Derrien wrote his Cinema Studies Master's thesis on TV series *Twin Peaks*, a choice that speaks volumes about the man.

In parallel with his studies, in Aix-en-Provence, he became editor-in-chief of *Rainbow Warrior*, a BD fanzine. Afterward he became scriptwriter for animated cartoons: the adaptations of *Blake & Mortimer*, *Spirou* and also *Bob Morane* and *Le Petit Nicolas*.

He also wrote episodes for original animated series such as *Kong*, *Xcalibur*, *Super 4*, *Skyland*, *Sonic Boom*, *Gormiti* and *Ernest & Rebecca*.

He recently wrote the hit comic book series *Frigiel and Fluffy*, based upon a Youtube phenomenon.

Beyond his work in comics, he also teaches scriptwriting at the ESRA Paris and SupdeCreation. He's currently working on several TV series and feature film projects as a writer.